This Camping Adventure

belongs to

Campground: _____   Date: _____

Location _____

We Stayed at Site # _____

Weather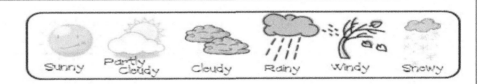

Sunny   Partly Cloudy   Cloudy   Rainy   Windy   Snowy

Memories:_____

_____

_____

_____

_____

The Best Camping Food_____

_____

 This Campground Was

Not great **X**   Average **X**   Good **X**   Amazing **X**

Camping Stories

Camping Stories

Camping Stories

Campground: _____ Date: _____

Location _____

We Stayed at Site # _____

Weather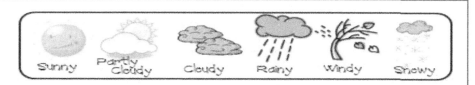

Sunny   Partly Cloudy   Cloudy   Rainy   Windy   Snowy

Memories:_____
_____
_____
_____
_____

The Best Camping Food_____
_____

 This Campground Was

Not great ✗   Average ✗   Good ✗   Amazing ✗

Camping Stories

Camping Stories

Camping Stories

Campground: _____ Date: _____

Location _____

We Stayed at Site # _____

Weather

Memories:_____
_____
_____
_____
_____

The Best Camping Food_____
_____

 This Campground Was

Not great **X**   Average **X**   Good **X**   Amazing **X**

Camping Stories

Camping Stories

Camping Stories

Campground: _____   Date: _____

Location _____

We Stayed at Site # _____

Weather

Memories:_____

_____

_____

_____

_____

The Best Camping Food_____

_____

   This Campground Was

Not great ✗   Average ✗   Good ✗   Amazing ✗

Camping Stories

Camping Stories

Camping Stories

Campground: _____   Date: _____

Location _____

We Stayed at Site # _____

Weather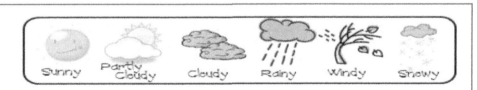

Sunny   Partly Cloudy   Cloudy   Rainy   Windy   Snowy

Memories:_____

_____

_____

_____

_____

The Best Camping Food_____

_____

 This Campground Was

Not great ✗   Average ✗   Good ✗   Amazing ✗

Camping Stories

Camping Stories

Camping Stories

 Campground: _____ Date: _____

Location _____

We Stayed at Site # _____

Weather

Memories:_____

_____

_____

_____

_____

The Best Camping Food_____

_____

 This Campground Was

Not great **X**   Average **X**   Good **X**   Amazing **X**

Camping Stories

Camping Stories

Camping Stories

 Campground: _____ Date: _____

Location _____

We Stayed at Site # _____

Weather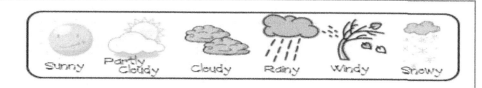

Sunny   Partly Cloudy   Cloudy   Rainy   Windy   Snowy

Memories:_____
_____
_____
_____
_____

The Best Camping Food_____
_____

 This Campground Was

Not great **X**   Average **X**   Good **X**   Amazing **X**

Camping Stories

Camping Stories

Camping Stories

 Campground: _____ Date: _____

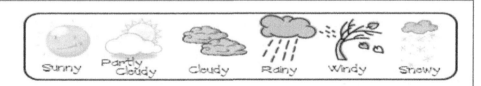

Location _____

We Stayed at Site # _____

Weather

Sunny Partly Cloudy Cloudy Rainy Windy Snowy

Memories:_____
_____
_____
_____
_____

The Best Camping Food_____
_____

   This Campground Was

Not great ✗   Average ✗   Good ✗   Amazing ✗

Camping Stories

Camping Stories

Camping Stories

Campground: _____ Date: _____

Location _____

We Stayed at Site # _____

Weather

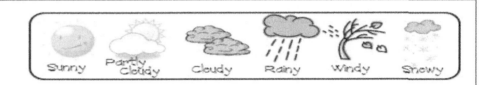

Sunny   Partly Cloudy   Cloudy   Rainy   Windy   Snowy

Memories:_____
_____
_____
_____
_____

The Best Camping Food_____
_____

This Campground Was

Not great **X**   Average **X**   Good **X**   Amazing **X**

Camping Stories

Camping Stories

Camping Stories

Campground: Date:

Location _____

We Stayed at Site # _____

Weather

Sunny   Partly Cloudy   Cloudy   Rainy   Windy   Snowy

Memories:_____
_____
_____
_____
_____

The Best Camping Food_____
_____

        This Campground Was

Not great **X**   Average **X**   Good **X**   Amazing **X**

Camping Stories

Camping Stories

Camping Stories

Campground: _____ Date: _____

Location _____

We Stayed at Site # _____

Weather

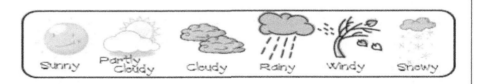

Sunny   Partly Cloudy   Cloudy   Rainy   Windy   Snowy

Memories:_____
_____
_____
_____

The Best Camping Food_____
_____

 ## This Campground Was

Not great **X**   Average **X**   Good **X**   Amazing **X**

Camping Stories

Camping Stories

Camping Stories

 Campground: _____   Date: _____

Location _____

We Stayed at Site # _____

Weather   Sunny   Partly Cloudy   Cloudy   Rainy   Windy   Snowy

Memories:_____

_____

_____

_____

_____

The Best Camping Food_____

_____

     This Campground Was

Not great ✗   Average ✗   Good ✗   Amazing ✗

Camping Stories

Camping Stories

Camping Stories

 Campground: _____ Date: _____

Location _____

We Stayed at Site # _____

Weather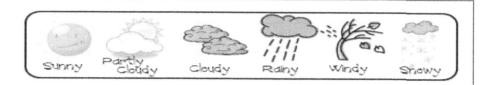
Sunny   Partly Cloudy   Cloudy   Rainy   Windy   Snowy

Memories:_____
_____
_____
_____
_____

The Best Camping Food_____
_____

This Campground Was

Not great **X**   Average **X**   Good **X**   Amazing **X**

Camping Stories

Camping Stories

Camping Stories

 Campground: _____ Date: _____

Location _____

We Stayed at Site # _____

Weather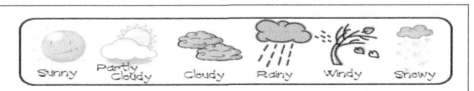
Sunny Partly Cloudy Cloudy Rainy Windy Snowy

Memories:_____
_____
_____
_____
_____

The Best Camping Food_____
_____

 This Campground Was

Not great ✗   Average ✗   Good ✗   Amazing ✗

Camping Stories

Camping Stories

Camping Stories

 Campground: _____ Date: _____

Location _____

We Stayed at Site # _____

Weather
Sunny   Partly Cloudy   Cloudy   Rainy   Windy   Snowy

Memories:_____
_____
_____
_____
_____

The Best Camping Food_____
_____

 This Campground Was

Not great ✗   Average ✗   Good ✗   Amazing ✗

Camping Stories

Camping Stories

Camping Stories

 Campground: _____ Date: _____

Location _____

We Stayed at Site # _____

Weather
Sunny Partly Cloudy Cloudy Rainy Windy Snowy

Memories:_____
_____
_____
_____
_____

The Best Camping Food_____
_____

 This Campground Was

Not great **X**   Average **X**   Good **X**   Amazing **X**

Camping Stories

Camping Stories

Camping Stories

Campground: _____ Date: _____

Location _____

We Stayed at Site # _____

Weather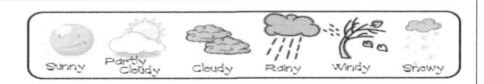

Sunny   Partly Cloudy   Cloudy   Rainy   Windy   Snowy

Memories:_____
_____
_____
_____
_____

The Best Camping Food_____
_____

 This Campground Was

Not great **X**   Average **X**   Good **X**   Amazing **X**

Camping Stories

Camping Stories

Camping Stories

 Campground: _____ Date: _____

Location _____

We Stayed at Site # _____

Weather
Sunny   Partly Cloudy   Cloudy   Rainy   Windy   Snowy

Memories:_____
_____
_____
_____
_____

The Best Camping Food_____
_____

 This Campground Was

Not great **X**   Average **X**   Good **X**   Amazing **X**

Camping Stories

Camping Stories

Camping Stories

Campground: _____ Date: _____

Location _____

We Stayed at Site # _____

Weather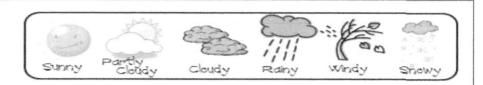

Sunny   Partly Cloudy   Cloudy   Rainy   Windy   Snowy

Memories:_____
_____
_____
_____
_____

The Best Camping Food_____
_____

 This Campground Was

Not great ✗   Average ✗   Good ✗   Amazing ✗

Camping Stories

Camping Stories

Camping Stories

 Campground: Date:

Location _____

We Stayed at Site # _____

Weather

Sunny   Partly Cloudy   Cloudy   Rainy   Windy   Snowy

Memories:_____

_____

_____

_____

_____

The Best Camping Food_____

_____

 This Campground Was

Not great **X**   Average **X**   Good **X**   Amazing **X**

Camping Stories

Camping Stories

Camping Stories

Campground: Date:

Location _____

We Stayed at Site # _____

Weather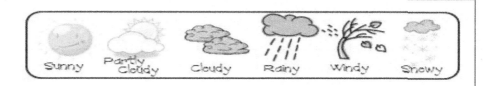

Memories:_____

_____

_____

_____

_____

The Best Camping Food_____

_____

 This Campground Was

Not great **X**   Average **X**   Good **X**   Amazing **X**

Camping Stories

Camping Stories

Camping Stories

Campground: Date:

Location _____

We Stayed at Site # _____

Weather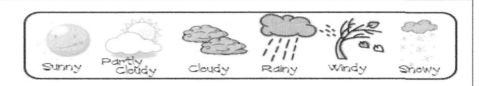

Sunny   Partly Cloudy   Cloudy   Rainy   Windy   Snowy

Memories:_____
_____
_____
_____
_____

The Best Camping Food_____
_____

    This Campground Was

Not great ✗   Average ✗   Good ✗   Amazing ✗

Camping Stories

Camping Stories

Camping Stories

 Campground: _____ Date: _____

Location _____

We Stayed at Site # _____

Weather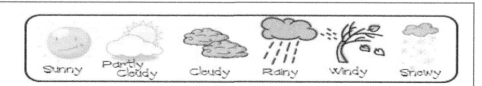

Sunny   Partly Cloudy   Cloudy   Rainy   Windy   Snowy

Memories: _____

_____

_____

_____

_____

The Best Camping Food _____

_____

 This Campground Was

Not great ✗   Average ✗   Good ✗   Amazing ✗

Camping Stories

Camping Stories

Camping Stories

Campground: _____   Date: _____

Location _____

We Stayed at Site # _____

Weather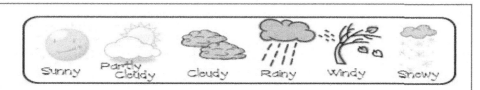

Sunny   Partly Cloudy   Cloudy   Rainy   Windy   Snowy

Memories:_____
_____
_____
_____
_____

The Best Camping Food_____
_____

 This Campground Was

Not great ✘   Average ✘   Good ✘   Amazing ✘

Camping Stories

Camping Stories

Camping Stories

Campground: _____ Date: _____

Location _____

We Stayed at Site # _____

Weather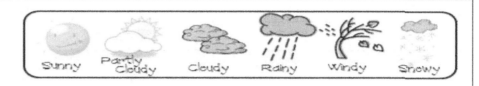
Sunny Partly Cloudy Cloudy Rainy Windy Snowy

Memories:_____

_____

_____

_____

_____

The Best Camping Food_____

_____

 This Campground Was

Not great ✗   Average ✗   Good ✗   Amazing ✗

Camping Stories

Camping Stories

Camping Stories

Campground: _____   **Date:** _____

Location _____

We Stayed at Site # _____

Weather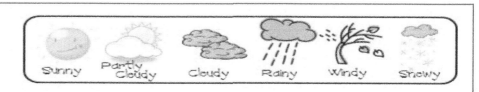

Memories:_____

_____

_____

_____

_____

The Best Camping Food_____

_____

     This Campground Was

Not great **X**   Average **X**   Good **X**   Amazing **X**

Camping Stories

Camping Stories

Camping Stories

 Campground: _____ Date: _____

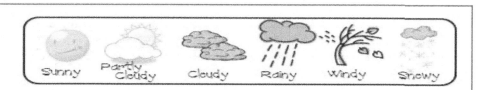

Location _____

We Stayed at Site # _____

Weather

Sunny | Partly Cloudy | Cloudy | Rainy | Windy | Snowy

Memories: _____
_____
_____
_____
_____

The Best Camping Food _____
_____

 This Campground Was

Not great ✗   Average ✗   Good ✗   Amazing ✗

Camping Stories

Camping Stories

Camping Stories